All Ways A Bridesmaid:

20 Rules Every Bridesmaid Should Follow

KATIE DUNNE

ALL WAYS A BRIDESMAID

CONTENTS

ALL WAYS A BRIDESMAID

ALL WAYS A BRIDESMAID

<u>WHY YOU SHOULD READ THIS BOOK</u>

Research shows that the average bridal party consists of five or six bridesmaids. Occasionally, they all know each other; sometimes, if they are lucky, they are all best friends. Some bridal parties consist of siblings, some are life long friends, some are new friends, and sometimes bridal parties are a motley crew from all walks of life, who hardly know each other at all.

The experience of being a bridesmaid can be pleasant, since it is all about celebration and drinking and dancing. However, it can also be a pain in the ass. In any case, if you are a bridesmaid (which I'm assuming you are, because you are reading this book) it is an experience you have found yourself in and you may be looking for some advice.

You are a chosen one, a bridesmaid. You have been picked by your friend, your sister, your future in-law (or whomever else is getting married), to be in their wedding; to stand next to them on the "best day of their life."

You have a brain full of expectations and so does your bride, but don't let the pressure get to you. There are many tasks ahead, but they can all be accomplished (and accomplished well) if you plan and communicate.

You may be expected to perform crazy tasks, you may be asked to do nothing at all, it all depends on who you are working with (the other 'maids) and who is getting married. You may encounter a slew of personalities; some will be fun, some will be bitchy, some you may even hate, but you have to deal with them all, at least until the wedding is over.

I, in the form of this book, am here to help. This book consists of advice, experience, and at least twenty rules every bridesmaid should follow.

If you take any piece of advice from this book, let it be: come from a place of love, and try to make whatever situation you are in, a good one for the bride. Your main role is to keep the bride happy, so remember that role in any scenario you find yourself in.

The path to someone else's alter is a bumpy one, dear bridesmaid. Hopefully, this book will make the journey a little bit smoother.

WHY I WROTE THIS BOOK

One rainy day in May, I went to the public library, which is my favorite place to be. I looked up "bridesmaid" in the digital catalog. *There was one book.*

I went to the section where the one book was supposed to be and I saw dozens of books for the bride, the occasional book for the groom, and plenty of magazines for wedding inspiration.

I continued my search and to my surprise, there were actually two books for bridesmaids on the shelf! Plus one book about giving toasts, so if you want to stretch it… there was a whopping three pieces of advice out there for you.

That is why I wanted to write this book. I think it is necessary, and my hope is that it will help at least one frustrated bridesmaid out there.

You may ask, "why is it necessary if there are already two books out there?!" Well, I skimmed those books and they are hundreds of pages long. They have advice for every personality and every event and every detail of every thing you might ever have to do. But guess what? That is a huge waste of time, and time is a commodity you don't have as a bridesmaid.

This book is short. It is sweet. It is to the point.

You can download all the checklists you want, but I am sharing real knowledge with you. Real things *every single bridesmaid* should keep in mind during this hectic time.

If you are looking for specific advice for your specific situation, there is probably a blog post for that. (Cough!...check out AllWaysABridesmaid.com...cough!)

Why should you take my advice? Let me introduce myself:

I am Katie Dunne, Founder of All Ways A Bridesmaid, and lover of love. I have been a bridesmaid so many times, I considered it my part-time job until I made it my actual job, via this book.

Once I reached the age where all of my friends started getting married, I was asked to be in most of their weddings. I've considered this is a great privilege and an honor. I love my friends. I love weddings. I love when my friends have weddings, and I love that they want me to be there standing next to them on their big day!

Being a part-time bridesmaid, I have seen a lot. I have been in bridal parties with cousins, friends, strangers, sorority sisters (the bride's, not mine), biological sisters (mine and/or the bride's) locals, out-of-towners, know-it-alls, bitches, goers-with-the-flow, cheapskates, and even girls who spend money like it's water. You name her… I've met her. So I've seen a lot and I think I have a lot of advice to give.

This book is full of real life stories from the weddings I have been in, chock full of life lessons that you may want to know about so you can avoid awkward situations before you encounter them, or so you know how to conquer them once you are in the thick of it.

The very first wedding I was in, was in 1988. Obviously back then my friends were not getting married, hell, I don't think I even had friends. I was two years old, and I was in my parents' wedding. I was the flower girl with the puffy 1980s style sleeves, smiling from ear to ear. I don't remember if I knew what was going on, I just knew I was staying up late eating cake, and life was good.

I rocked it back then, too. I didn't cry or fall asleep, I obviously didn't drink too much, and I helped the bride have a good time by hitting that dance floor with her.

(Hi, Mom!)

Fast forward to 2008. It had been twenty years since my first walk down the aisle, and I was asked to be a full-fledged bridesmaid for the first time in my sister's wedding. I think I rocked it then, too.

Since 2008 I have been in at least one wedding a year (sans 2014)…that's a lot of crinoline.

The rules I'm about to impart onto you have come from a decade of being a bridesmaid and seeing it all. Well, seeing a lot. Luckily I've never had to see anyone get left at the altar, or shoved in a pool in their wedding dress, or anything you might see during a Lifetime movie or a viral video. Believe me, though, I have been through a lot of the clichés that come along with being a bridesmaid, and I know how hard it can be.

If you follow the rules I lay out in this book, you will not only be a great bridesmaid, you will be the bride's favorite! You will also help keep the peace between yourself and the other bridesmaids, and, like I said before, make the walk down the aisle a smooth one.

You will be an old pro by the time you are in your second wedding, or third, or fourth…

One thing to keep in mind: everyone (and every bride) is different. These rules make sense for mostly every bridesmaid's journey, but not everyone will go through crazy drama. Not every path is bumpy.

I wish you luck on your walk down someone else's aisle, and know that I am always at AllWaysABridesmaid.com if you need me.

SOMETIMES YOU HAVE NO VOICE

There is a loud mouth in every group, am I right? It always seems like there is someone who feels like they have all the answers, like they don't need anyone else's input, and they know what is best for everyone.

Personally, my feelings about this person tend to flip flop. Sometimes I like the take charge attitude; sometimes I can't stand the bitch.

I am a shy person and the youngest of five, so having a say in most matters does not come easily for me. Going with the flow is part of my personality, but in certain situations, perhaps it shouldn't be. Let me explain.

The first time I was a bridesmaid, the wedding party I was a part of was full of biological sisters, sorority sisters, and ladies who knew the bride longer than the women who made up both of those other groups.

Who knew the bride best? If you asked everyone from that bridal party individually, we would have all said, "I do" (no pun intended). This I-know-what's-best mentality meant that personalities were bound to clash, people were bound to feel left out, and unanimous decisions were nearly impossible to make.

Full disclosure, this was my sister's wedding; the first wedding I was in as an adult, and I really had no idea what was expected of me. I was 22 years old and I put my trust in the older ladies of the group to figure things out. Many of them were married or had been a bridesmaid before, so I figured they knew what they were doing and they would just tell me what to do.

However, giving them all the power during the decision making process is something I wish I hadn't done.

I probably went with the flow too much during most discussions, and didn't allow my personality to show through enough. I could have helped more. I should have helped more. I've known my sister since I was born, damnit! I think I know her pretty well.

The fight that was brought up a lot was the one about money (a very common bridesmaid tiff, FYI). Living at my parents' and working full time allowed my bank account to grow to proper bridesmaid accountability, but I constantly felt like I was being asked to pay for things I had no say in.

Plus, when I asked for money for things I bought, I was looked down upon as if I had no idea what I was doing. I was younger than the rest of the ladies, but I felt like I was being looked at as the little sister too much, and that is not cool.

The major lesson I learned from this bridal party was to voice my ideas and opinions and not to go with the flow too much. I thought some of the ideas thrown around by others were terrible, so I should have said something.

Rule #1: *Allow everyone's voice to be heard*

Rule #2: *Don't allow yourself to be pushed to the back when you have something to contribute*

SOMETIMES YOU ARE THE
ONLY VOICE OF REASON

I once was in a small bridal party where it felt like no one could get their shit together, or really like no one wanted to. News flash: This happens a lot. People have lives to live and they can't spend all their time planning showers and bachelorette parties.

I am aware of this fact, but I still would have loved it if the bridal party, read: *bridal team* would have pitched in an idea or two.

I felt like the maid of honor didn't really understand the importance of her status, as she had never been part of a bridal party before. At the time, she was a very go-with-the-flow type of gal, and often hoped everything would fall into place. However, when planning things like bridal showers and bachelorette parties, you cannot hope everything just falls into place.

The bride wanted a semi-destination bachelorette party, meaning it would not be local, but we didn't need to buy plane tickets anywhere. We all said okay, and that was the extent of the planning…not good.

It was great that we knew we wouldn't disappoint in terms of the location of the bachelorette party, but in the execution? We could have done way better.

The maid of honor assumed we would just find things to do once we got to our destination, and you know what they say about people who assume: they make an "ass" out of "u" and "me."

The lack of planning led to disappointment throughout the bridal party and for the bride. Which makes me look back on the situation and think I should have stepped in and planned something better.

Even with little input from the rest of the bridal party, a quick Google search for "free things to do in (insert location)," or "things happening on (insert day of party)" would have helped when we hit the inevitable lull in the evening.

This bridal party experience made me feel like I failed as a bridesmaid. It is an upsetting thing when you fail as a bridesmaid, because you feel like you have also failed as a friend.

To make up for this snafu, we had a re-do party locally. We danced and drank and sang, and it was great. Now the bride can look back and see that we love her enough to have tried harder.

Plus, who doesn't love an extra fun night out with the girls?

Rule #3: *Over plan: having too many plans is better than no plans at all*

Rule #4: *Speak up when you see nothing is getting done*

EVERYONE LOVES A SURPRISE

I was in a bridal party where every suggestion I made, the maid of honor would go ask the bride if it was something she wanted. Even when I reiterated "and we can surprise her with" in my message. Pardon my language, but was she fucking kidding me?

This may be the most aggravated I've even been in a bridal party.

I understand that as a bridesmaid, you want to bride to have the best time, but I also understand that we are the circle of friends that knows the bride best. She doesn't need to know every detail of the planning process. In fact, she should not know the majority of it!

If you are in a bridal party with a bunch of other ladies, and one makes a suggestion that you are unsure of, go to the other bridesmaids first. *Not the bride.*

If the suggestion is, for example, a bouncy castle bachelorette party, and the bride told you just yesterday that she hates bouncy castles, the other girls should listen to your apprehensions and plan something different.

If the suggestion is something minor that you don't think the bride will like, but you think she can live with (like starting dinner at 4pm so everyone can go to bed by 10pm) maybe let it go. Tell the other girls your concerns, and if no one is on your side, then go with the flow and suck it up.

If there is no winning the fight for something you know the bride will absolutely hate (since "the stubborn bridesmaid" is a part of all of us) then and only then can you go to the bride and say something.

Then it's up to the bride to talk to the other girls about her distain for bouncy castles (or whatever the terrible detail is), and the bridesmaids will change the plans.

Please though, dear bridesmaid, don't let the bride plan her whole entire event. If she has ideas and is adamant about them, obviously implement them. But please do not go to her with every detail and ask if it is okay. She is entrusting you to know her enough to throw a great party. *Do that and more.*

If she says she wants strippers at her bachelorette party, get her a stripper. Do one further and surprise her with a lap dance.

If she says she wants to go wine tasting during her bachelorette party, go wine tasting. Do one further and surprise her with a cheese platter and a personalized wine glass when she arrives.

Everyone loves a surprise, even if that surprise is an enhancement on the party already hoped for in one's mind.

Rule #5: *Trust in the ideas of others*

Rule #6: *The bride should not know every little detail*

YOU MAY NOT EXPECT SOME THINGS

I'm going to be honest here. Sometimes surprises are good, sometimes they are not, and it completely depends on the situation.

Surprises that you know the bride will love? Great.

Surprises that sneak up on you? Not so great.

I was in my cousin's wedding in 2012, a cousin I have know my entire life, my built in best friend from birth.

Being chosen as her maid of honor was not something I expected, because she did have a BFF that she felt was better suited for the position, and I was totally cool with that.

However, I could have been a viable option, since we have know each other literally since the day I was born. So, it wasn't cool when the maid of honor stood up to give her speech and said something to the effect "I was chosen as your maid of honor, because who else could have been?"

Honestly, it struck me by surprise and offended me so greatly, I almost raised my hand (but I'm not an asshole).

When I said in the last section "Everyone Loves a Surprise" I was talking about the bride. Forget about the bride in this section though, because I want to talk about you, dear bridesmaid. I don't know if you are emotional or take things as personally as I do, but some things during this wedding journey may get to you.

Planning bridal showers and bachelorette parties may sound like fun, but in all honesty, it's stressful, hectic, and sometimes frustrating. You have all this new responsibility on top of work or school or home life, and it's taking up way more of your time than you may have expected.

It may feel like the other bridesmaids don't seem to be putting in as much effort as you, and you may feel like every suggestion they make will make the bride say, "what the hell is this?"

Just like a group project in high school, the worst part of being a bridesmaid is working with others.

Stress and frustration, especially in a group setting can often lead to explosions of emotions. While that sounds like a great name for an emo band, in reality, it sucks. It can lead someone in the bridal party to say hurtful things to you or others, and it may lead you to say things you don't mean, too.

The only advice I can give you for these situations is to think before you act and take a few deep breaths before speaking, so you don't punch anyone.

Rule #7: *Be careful what you say, because you could hurt someone's feelings*

Rule #8: *Don't take what people say to heart, they may not realize what they are saying*

CAN YOU JUST SHOW UP?

The short answer here is no.

The long answer here should also be no. You know what you signed up for, but let's talk about it for a bit.

Let's deep dive with a little role play. It's a Saturday night and your significant other asks where you would like to go for date night. You say, "I don't know, you pick." They say, "No, you pick." You go back and forth for a while and then you just get so hungry, you order in and rent a movie. If this scenario has even happened in your life, you may be the type of bridesmaid that asks if you can just show up.

Or you may ask if you can just throw money at whatever everyone else comes up with because you are too busy to help plan.

News flash: we are all busy. And most of us don't want to plan anything; especially a party for someone else.

If you want to just show up or just throw money in the pot, you are likely not married. I say this because I know that a woman who has been a bride before knows that the walk down the aisle starts way before you arrive at the chapel. It starts with the proposal, continues on to the engagement party, then the asking of ladies to be your bridesmaids, the bridal shower, bachelorette party, and finally the wedding.

Every piece is special, especially now that we have to post everything on social media. I mean, people have hashtags for every event in their life. If there is nothing to show on social media, did it actually really happen?

I'm kidding about that, of course. Your whole life doesn't have to be broadcasted, but I assure you, these events will live in the memory of a bride for a long time. Therefore, planning them and planning them well, is important.

Much like life, getting married is a journey, not a destination. If this sounds super dramatic to you, I assume again, you have never been married.

I have friends who have been married for almost ten years and they still bring up their bachelorette parties and bridal showers. You remember these milestones on the wedding journey because they are all important.

They let you know that the people you have chosen to share this momentous occasion with know you well enough to make the lead up to the big day super special.

Don't just show up, don't just give money. Spend a couple hours of your life thinking about the bride's wishes and make these events special. She will thank you for your effort.

Rule #9: *Brides have high expectations for every part of the wedding journey*

Rule #10: *Care enough to show the bride know you care a lot*

AGE ISN'T JUST A NUMBER

You may have some younger people in the bridal party, and this is something you have to think about. I mentioned before that being treated like the little sister of the group is not fun, but you may have to consider the "little sister bridesmaid" in certain situations.

One of my best friend got married in 2009. She was the first of our friends to tie the knot, and we were relatively young at the time. The bridal activities may have reflected that fact, in terms of our budget, our knowledge of planning, and our experience.

Her sister-in-law helped plan most of the bachelorette party, and she may have even picked up the slack money-wise, but I don't really remember how much it all cost; I just remember most of the bridal party made retail salaries, so money did not flow very freely.

The reason her bachelorette party worked for everyone involved was because we knew what we were getting into, and we knew how to plan accordingly.

For example, one thing we did was stay local. We went out to eat, went to a wine bar, went to a place that had karaoke, and it was a good time! We even had a designated driver, in order to save money on a limo or other public transportation.

Even though the were young (and sometimes the younger you are the harder you party), I don't think we got too rowdy.

There were penis straws involved, obviously, but I think due to budget and time, it may have been the most subdued bachelorette party I've been a part of. Which was perfect, as the bride was not a rowdy partier.

Younger bridesmaids may not have the financial means to help out as much as others can, and if this is your situation, you should to speak up about it. You can make more inexpensive location suggestions, or you can have a personal budget in mind to cap what you spend on food and drinks while you are out on the town.

You also never know who is willing to compromise until you ask. Plans can change to meet everyone's financial needs, or other bridesmaids might be willing to pitch in more because they, for example, want to see that stripper dance, and they just got a nice bonus at work that will pay for it.

If no one wants to compromise, you may have to sit out of the bachelorette party. If this is the case, you should tell the bride personally, so she knows where you are coming from and that you still love her.

Rule #11: *Younger 'maids often go with the flow, because they don't know what they are doing*

Rule #12: *If you are not financially ready to contribute, talk to the other bridesmaids about your situation*

YOUR TRADITION IS NOT EVERYONE'S TRADITION

I can't tell you how many times I've heard something like, "During my sister's bridal shower we did this." And I can't tell you how many times the snarky bitch in my brain said, "No one cares, this isn't your sister's bridal shower."

Luckily my mouth has the much-needed filter my brain does not.

I was in a bridal party one time where we didn't go dress shopping together. This is one of my favorite wedding activities, but it obviously isn't as important to others as it is to me.

I will reiterate over and over again that everyone is different and they like or do different things, and that should be respected.

Some brides are so nonchalant that they can pick a dress and have all of the bridesmaids order it online. They can check that off of the mountain of to-dos and be super happy about it.

You, as a bridesmaid must deal with it. Don't beg for things, don't ask the bride to do things more than once (unless she is flaky and it's something important and necessary like getting a marriage license).

Some things a bride chooses to do may offend you, but I tell you this with love: You aren't the one getting married, so shut up. A few things on the list of "why would she do that? I would never," include but are not limited to:

- A bride who is not religious getting married in a church
- A bride who wears a see-through gown
- A bride who all of the sudden embraces the fact she is 4% Italian and must have cannolis for dessert
- A bride with too many preferences
- A bride with no preferences at all

- A bride who begs to know every detail of the party planning process
- A bride who hands over all reigns to her maid of honor
- A bride who wants to get married on a weeknight
- A bride who sees her groom before walking down the aisle
- A bride who does or does not care about anything borrowed, old, new, or blue
- A bride who talks about how much money certain things like her ring or the reception cost
- A bride who drinks too much champagne the day of the wedding (although you should stop this before it gets out of hand)
- A bride who gets cold feet

There are many more things a bride can do in this hyper-sensitive time. She may yell at you for something stupid, she may forget to do things that you've ask her to do, she may start talking about her high school sweetheart who was "the one that got away."

As a bridesmaid, you are there to listen and offer support. She has not right to hurt your feelings, but keep her feelings in mind as well. Just keep reminding yourself that weddings make people crazy, and this will all be over soon.

Rule #13: *Some brides embrace traditions you would not expect during this big life change*

Rule #14: *You do not have the right to judge...at least not out loud*

KNOW YOUR BRIDE

I once had a bride show me a picture and said she wanted it to be the theme of her shower. This wasn't merely a suggestion, it was a request. A this-better-be-a-part-of-my-shower request.

You better believe that picture was in my memory bank, and perhaps on my "Bridal Shower" Pinterest board for future reference.

Some people may think that move was very "bridezilla" of her, but if you were getting married and you had a vision, you would share it with your friends too. Or at least you should.

As a bridesmaid, imagine if you come up with a whole bridal shower theme that you are excited about. You've got every little detail perfect, and you can't wait until the bride shows up. You have the big reveal and the bride gives an exasperated sigh, because she had envisioned something completely different. You would be upset, right?

You would be sad that the bride is disappointed in your hard work, and may even be mad that she didn't give you any ideas to work with. So, if your bride hands you a picture, or sends you her dream shower Pinterest board, look at it and use it. It will make her happy, and your life easier.

And, as you know dear bridesmaid, *your only job is to make her happy*.

Knowing your bride matters in all stages of the journey down the aisle.

For example, if you are dress shopping and you know your bride takes things personally, don't put on a dress and immediately tell her you despise it. If she spent the time to pick it out, she will fell like you despise her, even though she had nothing to do with creating the dress.

You also have to know your bride while planning the bachelorette party. Not everyone wants a drunken night on the town or stripper poles.

I know I have said to keep things a surprise, but I also will give this piece of advice: if the bridal party cannot decide on themes or activities, it is okay to ask the bride something like, "if you look back on you bachelorette party, what would make you so happy to see?" or "what would you be disappointed without?"

Her answer may be vague, or it may be specific, but either way it will leave you something to work with.

My answer to those questions was drag queens. My wish was granted, I didn't know any other plan, and I was a very happy bride.

Rule #15: *If the bride wants something specific, incorporate it the best way you can*

Rule #16: *It is okay to ask the bride what she absolutely wants if the choices are overwhelming*

THE ONE GOAL OF EVERY BRIDESMAID

The one goal of every bridesmaid is to help where ever and when ever you can. You are not a bride's maid, but you are her friend, her support system, and her helper. However, you have the right to say no.

Some brides seem to take their bridal authority and go absolutely ape shit about it, thinking they have built in servants for a few months. This is not the truth.

A wedding day is very important. *I will totally give you that.* A bride plans for months or years, she spends a ton of money on a four hour party that flies by in what feels like minutes. She wants the whole journey to be perfect. However, I don't condone "bridezilla" behavior at all.

If I were someone's friend for years, and as soon as they asked me to be in their wedding they became a monster who dictated every little detail, I would flip out.

Weddings are a time to celebrate friends, not loose them because they dislike the dress you picked out for them. (Oh, P.S. If you don't like the dress, but she picks it, you are wearing it regardless.)

Be accommodating and nice to the bride, but maybe talk about it later with your fellow bridesmaids. I know it seems a little "Mean Girl"-ish to talk behind the bride's back, but keeping the peace is one of the most important things you can do.

Again, everyone is different...People handle stress in totally different ways. On top of her job and her home life, a bride has to plan a party for hundreds of people.

She has to remember to plan every detail. She feels like she has to out-do every other wedding she has ever been to (at least this is how some brides think). She has to remember the marriage license, pick the perfect dress, confirm with the florist and caterer...

Plus, have you ever made a seating chart? It's insane. And so stressful.

It is totally understandable that women go a little crazy during this time in their lives. However, it is not an excuse to be a total bitch; especially to your best friends.

You, dear bridesmaid, have rights. You have the right to sit your bride down and tell her that she's being a little mean or that she's going nuts. You have to say this with grace and love, of course, but it may save your friendship.

It also may open her eyes to how psycho she is being and may lead her to find a bit of zen and stress less. That's a win, win.

I'm sharing with you what I've learned throughout my years. Maybe your bride actually needs a slap in the face. Maybe she needs to talk it out. Maybe she really wants your opinion. You know her better than I do. See Rule #17 and do your best.

Rule #17: *Be helpful how ever you can be*

Rule #18: *Keep the peace when ever possible*

THE GOLDEN RULE

The golden rule of bridesmaiding is to know your role. Honestly, the type of bridesmaid you are, kind of depends on the type of bride you are working with and who the other bridesmaids are. You may have a sense pretty early on which role you need to play.

Being a bridesmaid is an honor and a privilege; it means your friend or relative loves you enough to include you in a huge milestone celebration. It means they trust you enough to show them a good time when it comes to the pre-wedding festivities like bridal showers and bachelorette parties.

Being a bridesmaid is also an investment. You need to be ready and willing to spend your money on the parties, the dresses, the gifts, etc. You also need to be ready to spend your time with the bride in times of crisis (or over dramatic flare ups). You may even have to be crafty and help build their centerpieces or bake cupcakes.

Like I've mentioned in other parts of this book, being on team bride is like working on a group project in high school. You may not want to do it, you may not like the people you have to work with, but it is 50% of your grade…I mean it is a big part of your relationship with the bride.

You love her, so show up and do the work and reward yourself with the open bar at the wedding.

At times bridesmaiding might be frustrating, but it can also be a lot of fun if you indeed know your role and know when to step back.

People are fighting in the group text message? Turn on do not disturb and take a bubble bath. Go back to it when you are good and relaxed.

Another bridesmaid hates your ideas? Take a deep breath and say, "I see where you are coming from, but we need to plan for the bride, and I know she will love what I've suggested."

It's even better if you don't mind if your plans change. Be the ultimate flow-goer (when it's right) and say, "Fine. You plan it," and walk away.

This may sound hypocritical to some of the other advice I've given, but if someone is really fighting you on something, their misery is not worth your time or energy. (You should obviously fight the idea if you know the bride will hate it, but) if you hate their idea just because it is different from yours, go with it and relax.

There are some amazing things about being a bridesmaid. You get to play dress up! You get to go out dancing or have a slumber party during the bachelorette party! You get to drink so much champagne and wine and eat so much cake!

You get to spend more time with your friend than you probably ever will again after she is married. You get to celebrate life and friendship and most of all love. Embrace your role as bridesmaid, and you will enjoy the journey, too.

Rule #19: *Go with the flow when you can*

Rule #20: *Remember to celebrate the love*

TO RECAP

The bride has the most stressful journey down the aisle, but the bridesmaid is a close second. However, I think being a bridesmaid is truly a privilege and it really is a time to be embraced. If you are feeling overwhelmed or burdened by it, I hope these 20 rules gave you a reason to flip your thought process and being a bridesmaid is something you are ready for and excited about now!

If you need further advice or have specific questions you need answered (or even need to vent about someone) you can write to **hello@allwaysabridesmaid.com** and we can totally chat.

Thanks for reading!

-Katie

52

ABOUT THE AUTHOR

Back in the day, Katie Dunne thought she wanted to be an event planner. The idea of spending someone else's money to throw lavish events enticed her greatly. She started her career and it wasn't what she thought it would be (but that's a story for a different time).

She began concentrating on the events that she loved the most, and they included smaller, more intimate gatherings, like bridal and baby showers, and that's where her empathy for frustrated bridesmaids began.

She understands the struggle because she has been there and done that, in the decade worth of weddings she was able to be a part of. She has dealt with all sorts of bridesmaids, and can relate to them all on some level.

She also believes that to share your knowledge is one way to change the world. That is why this book was born.

Katie Dunne loves love. She thinks weddings are the best parties out there. She likes being a guest, and loves being a bridesmaid.